MEGA-CITIES IN THE TROPICS

The **Institute of Southeast Asian Studies** was established as an autonomous organization in May 1968. It is a regional research centre for scholars and other specialists concerned with modern Southeast Asia, particularly the multi-faceted problems of stability and security, economic development, and political and social change.

The Institute is governed by a twenty-two-member Board of Trustees comprising nominees from the Singapore Government, the National University of Singapore, the various Chambers of Commerce, and professional and civic organizations. A ten-man Executive Committee oversees day-to-day operations; it is chaired by the Director, the Institute's chief academic and administrative officer.

The **Social Issues in Southeast Asia (SISEA)** programme was established at the Institute in 1986. It addresses itself to the study of the nature and dynamics of ethnicity, religions, urbanism, and population change in Southeast Asia. These issues are examined with particular attention to the implications for, and relevance to, an understanding of problems of development and of societal conflict and co-operation. SISEA is guided by a Regional Advisory Board comprising senior scholars from the various Southeast Asian countries. At the Institute, SISEA comes under the overall charge of the Director while its day-to-day running is the responsibility of the Co-ordinator.

MEGA-CITIES IN THE TROPICS
TOWARDS AN ARCHITECTURAL AGENDA FOR THE FUTURE

TAY KHENG SOON

ISEAS

SOCIAL ISSUES IN SOUTHEAST ASIA
INSTITUTE OF SOUTHEAST ASIAN STUDIES

This publication is based on a seminar presented on 29 March 1989 at the Institute of Southeast Asian Studies, chaired by Professor K.S. Sandhu of the Institute.

Published by
Institute of Southeast Asian Studies
Heng Mui Keng Terrace
Pasir Panjang
Singapore 0511

Cataloguing in Publication Data

Tay, Kheng Soon.
    Mega-cities in the tropics : towards an architectural agenda for the future.
    1.   Architecture—Tropics.
    2.   City planning—Tropics.
    I.   Institute of Southeast Asian Studies (Singapore)
    II.   Title.
    NA2541 T23   1989   sls89-69915

ISBN 981-3035-33-1

Printed in Singapore by Loi Printing Pte. Ltd.

CONTENTS

ACKNOWLEDGEMENT

The preparation of *Mega-Cities in the Tropics* was made possible with the financial assistance of the Volkswagen Foundation. The Institute of Southeast Asian Studies would like to thank the Foundation for its support. However, the study remains the responsibility of the author and his views do not necessarily reflect those of the Foundation or the Institute.

MEGA-CITIES IN THE TROPICS

Ecologically balanced small towns and settlements in the tropics or the equatorial belt became the mega-cities of today due to modernization and modern medicine. We are talking about cities like Caracas, Bombay, Singapore, Manila, Jakarta, Bangkok, and so forth. These are today mega-cities of 3 million and above. And they came about because they broke the pattern established by the natural regime imposed on life in the tropics by death and disease. Tropical cities without modernization cannot support the population densities that now exist. The acceleration of growth was due to modernization initiated by colonization. This impetus grew further after the transfer of power to national élites after World War II. Plantations, resource exploitation, and colonial trade provided the initial push; industrialization and systematic administration pushed it further. Those who could organize their political systems around the network of international interdependencies grew faster and fared better than those who did not. None the less, the intense concentration of populations in these cities in the mean while benefited from advances in tropical hygiene and the introduction of urban infrastructure and public services. It is worth remembering that during the early nineteenth century, smallpox for example, killed off half a million people in and around the Jakarta area within two weeks. And of course tropical hygiene was first propelled by colonial interests and indeed today the centre of tropical hygiene is still in London and Edinburgh. But town planning lagged behind — it is still based on northern models and adapted *ad hoc* in response to new economic and social conditions. Today we have new industrial estates, public housing estates, and free-trade zones, but they are modified from their northern models.

There were adaptations in the developing countries but no basic review. Thus today we have the mega-cities in the tropics but have yet to realize the potentials of tropical living in cities because there has not been any basic review of the inherited town-planning doctrines and concepts. Indeed, virtually all our town planners in the tropical region are educated in northern universities and are totally immersed in the doctrines of northern town planning. Although there has been some interest in tropical architecture, this did not extend into planning. This interest was propelled by British consultancy jobs in Africa in the 50s and 60s. The interest in tropical architecture, however, concentrated only on individual buildings. There was hardly any new ideas regarding the whole city or the tropical environment of urban areas as such. So there has been a gap at the conceptual level in the planning of dense tropical urban environments. Tropical architecture as a discipline virtually became defunct because the implied architectural style became dated and because the design of tropical buildings as individual buildings did not really solve the noise, dust, and heat problems which are created by the city itself, and which no single building can hope to solve except by air-conditioning. Tropical architecture is, however, applicable in suburban conditions but is too limited to solve environmental and climatic problems in city centres. The reliance on air-conditioning has become the only way of ameliorating environmental and climatic problems. The other issue is that city design is still considered as a passive vehicle for economic development. Planning is aimed at providing a platform for economic development, transportation, and housing. Planning has not been conceived of as being capable of stimulating new products

*HT may well stimulate a lot of new activities with economic social impact or might be better-designed business places,

* Idea for social design – Remind residents to insist on comparable-to-HT planning where they work & to protect if the "passive vehicle" model is used.

and new economic activities in addition to the traditional economic activities.

That town planning can stimulate new products and new businesses I will show later. In terms of industrialization, the economy of cities in the tropics are import-substituting and also function mainly as foreign production and financial bases. Nothing intrinsic has come out of city planning in the tropics thus far. There are of course other geo-political reasons for this — and I am not equipped to discuss these — but I will concentrate mainly on physical planning and its architectural implications. That this thought might, however, stimulate a new consciousness of tropical potentials is hoped. This is the historic challenge for Singapore since it is the most developed city in the tropical belt in terms of having a well-organized urban infrastructure, administration, professional system, and highly organized as compared with many other cities in the tropics. And then there are other factors — and these are new developments in transportation, telecommunications, and more recently information technology (IT). These new factors are having an impact on life in all cities, whether in the tropics or elsewhere. Therefore, how these developments can influence the conceptualization of the tropical city is the question that we need to address. The Historic Agenda is therefore the liberation of tropical cities' inherent potentials — tropical design augmented by built-in information systems combined with a lively civic urban culture should create a new civilization capable of releasing unused potentials in the people as well as the environment. Besides extensive use of electronic information systems the tropical city must provide for heightened human contact. Spaces must be provided and

— *important general point that this "civic urban culture" not be just designed for rich dudes, leaving the rest to fend...*

an open civic urban culture be allowed to grow. This is the scope of the Urban Agenda urged by our age. Singapore is well placed to address this agenda perhaps better than most cities since many of the others are beset with steamy congestion exacerbated by intense social conflicts, endemic poverty, and great disparities threatening to tear their social fabric part. Given such a situation it is hardly possible to think fundamentally about tropical city planning while attending to day-to-day problems. What we do in Singapore therefore could have impacts beyond our shores and give us a role in the tropical world which goes beyond mere South-South and North-South rhetoric. When we start to think about developing our city as a tropical city, we will derive concepts, technologies, and products which initially we will need for ourselves but which later can be made available to others.

Focus on the Intelligent Tropical City arose simultaneously from several agendas which have converged in the last five years. The aspect of "intelligence" came from developments in the IT field. Concepts such as information science, teleworking, interactive television, hyper-media, artificial intelligence, and expert systems have spurred speculation, experimentation, and research into human interfaces — the family and the community — implications on leisure, learning, work, and automated production.

Impetus on IT's impact on physical planning is relatively new and it is best illustrated by the Kawasaki Advanced Information City International Competition organized in 1986. When Kawasaki, an obsolete, heavy-industry, fringe-city of Tokyo, agreed to be the site for a national experi-

Relevant to HT ála Toffler.

ment as an Advanced Information City in 1986, it drew world-wide participation. Kawasaki city was conceptualized as a campus city offering continuing education, leisure, and learning for all its citizens as well as addressing thirty-seven topics and issues related to what life ought to be like in the twenty-first century. The Kawasaki Advanced Information City International Competition threw up tremendous amounts of ideas, the ramifications of which are still being debated. The competition was won by an MIT group. Just to keep you abreast of the developments, the Japanese are investing in the building of an information city in Australia and the MIT group is involved in the conceptualization of that. The same group has also been appointed to study the future of Washington. And many of these ideas are relevant to Singapore. And I would like to show you some of them later in the slides. The other main value of the Kawasaki exercise was the intense dialogue stimulated during the run-up to the competition in Japan itself in which Japanese intellectual, professional, technological, and conceptual resources were poured into the project brief. Typically, the Japanese have a broad-base approach and they fund out their ideas and thinking over the four-year period spent on this project. So by the time the Kawasaki project was launched, a huge consensus had already developed throughout many institutions. I will show you the structure of who were involved and you can then appreciate the extent of the Japanese commitment. We need to do the same here if the Intelligent Tropical City concept is to be developed in depth.

The idea of an information city is of course not new. There have been research, writing, and speculation over the last twenty years and a considerable literature exists to draw from. As Singapore embarks on high-quality production, high-tech industry, and an extensive IT network, the issues raised in Kawasaki are of special relevance to us. And perhaps what is in our favour is that we can take advantage of these new ideas faster than others because of our compactness.

IT impact should therefore be considered in physical planning. It could mean new kinds of dwellings and new kinds of neighbourhoods, new patterns of multiple land and building use which stimulate more social skills needed by the growing information culture. IT has always been not just a hardware issue, but a software issue as well. The human factor is crucial. Effective IT use requires it to mimic human processes and augment human activities. The displacement of human labour by machines also places a greater demand on the human ability to formulate questions, form concepts, and take initiatives. More is expected of the worker than merely taking orders and performing accurately repetitive tasks designated by his superior. The human being thus has to be master of whatever situation he is in. The challenges a family, a society, and educational institutions face are tremendous. The human being becomes less a tool in the production process but more a thinking, feeling, sensing, and intuiting being. The implications are enormous. Social mores, customary role expectations will change accordingly.

The aspect of tropicality, however, arose regionally. It came out of a series of discussions which started in Kuala Lumpur. Originally they were hosted by Pertubahan Akitek Malaysia, which is the Institute of Architects in Kuala Lumpur, under the leadership of one Ken Yeang. The discussions were spurred by the architectural identity quest stimulated by the government, which desired a Malaysian identity in architecture. And various senior government members actually said at the conference I attended that if architects didn't come up with a Malaysian identity in design, then the government would have to tell architects what to do. This alarmed the whole profession because everybody could see Minangkabau roofs coming up all over the place. The government was impatient with the slow pace of the development of visible symbols of Malaysian identity. This challenge took hold not only for that reason; it was also propelled by a disquiet — I could sense a disquiet amongst Malaysian architects at an implied ethnic sectarianism in the choice of ethnic symbols. That is one aspect of the problem. The other is that it took hold also because of tendencies among architects to follow the lead of architects in the developed world, who have a different set of problems but who are none the less searching for new stylistic approaches in North America and Europe and to some extent in Japan, in response to a perceived paradigm shift away from the corporate industrial values which the West is experiencing.

This shift was identified and led by philosophers and literary figures in the 60s and 70s, in what can be broadly described as post-industrialism, deconstructionism, and post-modernism. On post-industrialism, I think the seminal works of people like Daniel Bell, romantics like Theodore Roszak, and of course in Europe the intellectual drive especially in the literary field came from people like Foucault and Derrida and their critic Jurgen Herbemas. So what we have now is a ferment of ideas questioning the basis of industrial values and industrial society itself. And out of this ferment has come a shaking up of the architectural paradigms too which are, after all, a response to the industrial paradigm itself. So in this situation, we are facing a period of uncertainty and disorientation resulting in what can be described as an eclectic period in architecture.

In line with this eclectic phase of the so-called post-modernist architecture in the West, Asian architects are also beginning to incorporate their own ethnic and cultural symbols in their building designs. This is historically absurd; it is also dangerous because it inadvertently exacerbates ethnic cleaveages that lie just below the surface of new-state cultures. And you can see some of the evidence of ethnicity in style already in Singapore. Quite a number of HDB (Housing and Development Board) estates are beginning to look Chinese and there are public buildings that look Malay or Indian. And the game is a dangerous one. In Malaysia, Taiwan, Korea, and especially in the embattled Arab Islamic nations — and I have some knowledge of the Arab Islamic situation because of my involvement with the Aga Khan programme — these nations which are undergoing rapid change also face the problem of how to be modern and yet have a unique cultural identity of their own. Because to be modern would imply adopting Western technology and Western styles, dress as well as building styles which are becoming ubiquitous. The homogenizing process is taking place everywhere, and especially at the visual level. And that is something which is regretted by identity-conscious new states. But, as an artistic enterprise, the idea of incorporating ethnic symbols in modern buildings to make them different and identifiable has on the whole been unsatisfactory. The architectural results appear contrived. The dilemma is real. And because of this the national architectural identity discourse which started in Kuala Lumpur in 1986 stalled. It then began to shift its focus to a search for a regional expression rather than an ethnic expression. Now, it is in this context that there is a need for a more intrinsic design agenda for tropical Asian countries. And that is to seek the design agenda from the environment itself, which is specific to place and time. In architecture and urban planning, the pragmatics and the poetics of place are the neglected potentials of geography and history. The new technological environment can also be brought in as a generator of form and expression and to create a sense of cohesive identity which transcends ethnicity and culture. This is the challenge to the creative design professions.

Thinking on the Intelligent Tropical City therefore sprang from this background. The Intelligent Tropical City concepts juxtapose IT with economics, culture, and geography in urban settings. Here we are not talking about suburban or rural settings where the environment is not debilitating, as is the case in dense cities. We are talking of dense urban settings where heat and humidity are endemic conditions which need to be ameliorated at the environmental planning level before it reaches the building stage. I will show you some of the climatic measurements done in Kuala Lumpur by Dr Sham Sani of the Geography Department, University of Malaya, which attest to the phenomenon of the "heat island effect".

The Tropical City concept seeks to utilize positively the rain, the sun, the wind, and the vegetation to produce a conducive and efficient living environment *imaginatively*. Up to now the response to the tropical environment has basically been negative rather than positive. Negative in

PLANT NETS

PLANT NETS

26°C

IDEAL
+ 26°C
MAYBE
28°C

SHADES. + EVAPORATIVE
COOLING.

+ 30°C
OPEN FIELD
AMBIENT TEMP.
IN STILL AIR
CONDITION.

THE IDEAL IS TO REPLICATE THE TROPICAL FOREST CONDITION.

the sense of avoiding the sun and avoiding the rain. That of course is only one aspect of the problem. You have a building here at ISEAS that you can't enter without getting wet because the shelter stops just short of the road. There is no canopy over the road. And you cannot extend beyond the road because the laws prevent you from extending beyond the road. Why are the laws that way? Because the laws are not responsive to the tropical environment. So property lines become the definer of limits of extension and they become what defines the environment rather than the environment stimulating the production of laws that allow forms to respond properly. So we have this problem right here. And of course a new life-style is obviously implied too — linkage and connectivity are the key words. Now the poetic agenda which I think architects and creative people are particularly interested in is how to embody that which is unique and intrinsic in the tropics. So we are not talking about just an engineering approach or an administrative approach to the problem of designing cities and buildings in the tropics. We are talking about poetic and rhapsodic dimensions as well. And the issue is also how to create a poetic image of tropical cities and buildings that can be enchanting, that captivates, and that enhances attachment and love for the place despite the density in the cities. For Singapore this translates into what Lord Norwich distilled in his book *A History of Venice*: Venice's twin strategy of expanding business opportunities and creating enchantment simultaneously. Venice was not just a business centre. Venice was also a tremendously artistic and beautiful place. And this strategy of course ensured Venice's pre-eminence in the Mediterranean for over 1,000 years in commerce, ideas, and in the arts.

And this is particularly pertinent for island city-states like Singapore. We should adopt such a strategy taking into account the specific characteristics of Singapore.

The rest of this paper lists some suggested agendas which arise from the theme. The purpose is to outline the scope of the inquiry involved and the extent of multi-disciplinary research and development that will ensue. The overall method is to build a consensus and to stimulate research prior to implementation since there is no precedent for the Intelligent Tropical City concept. And I am very happy to read the Minister for National Development's speech published on the seventeenth of this month about building the great Equatorial City, noting that it has no precedent. And the lack of precedent is a challenge for creative thinking. A lot more work has to be done. Looking around this room I would say that this is the group to do it. Who else is going to do it? And we need to start preparations early so that when it is time to build, we will not have to resort again to ready-made imported concepts and ideas just because we have not done our homework. Singapore will never be a first-class city if it cannot initiate basic and fundamental ideas on what it is and what it can become. Singapore will always remain in my mind a second-class, provincial town with global pretentions if it is not able to focus on the specifics and poetics of place.

Now, I am aware of course that some of the agenda items are already being investigated by different people for different purposes. What is needed, I feel, is to draw them together into a coherent and overall theme so that a shared vision can arise. I think a concerted multi-disciplinary team of conceptualizers, technologists, administrators, and professionals

is needed to advance the ideas outlined here. There has to be some kind of focus, some kind of intensity in the approach.

I'd like to list down very quickly the agenda headings now.

The Historic Agenda
Building the great tropical city is a response to the potentials of our time and the specifics of our place. It is also a challenge to integrate ethics, societal values, and cultural proclivities through a clear collective vision that works. It fulfills the promise of our place and time. It unties the intellectual umbilical cords.

The International Agenda
1 Global environment
    — clean energy
    — ecological balance
    — water pollution control
    — air pollution control
2 North-South dialogue and the South-South dialogue — the expansion of real opportunities beyond rhetoric
3 Modern Asian identity and Singapore's role in relation to other tropical cities — technological transfers and conceptual relevance
4 Asian democracy and civic urban culture — dialogue and participation through a shared vision
5 Focus on new developmental paradigms — integration of fragmented life, work, and learning

6 Aid and fair trade — expansion of South-South and North-South trade and regional complementation

The Strategic Planning Agenda
1 Compact planning — high intensity and multiple uses
2 Historic conservation — protection and enlargement of scope
3 Nature conservation — inventory and audit
4 Transport modelling, planning, and management
5 Water resource modelling, development, and management
6 Energy audit and modelling for development and management
7 Floor and land space allocation — as a function of the national agenda and vision
8 Time budgetting and optimization — world perspective — 24-hour city
9 Night-time uses and work/leisure schedules and infrastructural support
10 Family/learning and earning — family life cycle strategy
11 Rural/urban relations — balanced developments
12 Disaster planning
13 Place attachment — psychology of place
14 Participation process — consensus, debate, new ideas, conceptual review
15 Open planning discourse — structure and accessibility
16 Clean air policy
17 Clean river policy
18 Clean sea policy

19 Topography conservation
20 Co-ordinated planning — a multi-agency approach — public and private sector partnership
21 Specific operational ideologies *vis-à-vis* various production and economic realms
22 Total environmental accounting — costs, benefits, and disbenefits
23 Price structuring

The Urban Design Agenda
1   Volumetric modelling
2   Geometric modelling
3   Vertical zoning
4   Infill developments
5   Connectivity — physical, visual, and thematic — horizontal and vertical linkages
6   Synergistic mix of uses and social choreography
7   Synergistic infrastructure
8   Landscaping and building mix strategy
9   Transport and mobility — choices and consequences
10 Utilization of sun, wind, and water
11 Urban cognition and identity — design strategies
12 Incrementality in services and urban systems
13 Noise, dust pollution controls
14 Synergistic urban ecological systems — policies and proposals

15 Micro climate creation
16 Bridging structures between buildings

The Architectural Agenda

1 Buildings as support frames for human activity and living nature — architecture as support structure — architecture as landscape
2 Rainwater collection and recycling as part of building design
3 Refuse collection and recycling
4 Vertical landscaping — provision and upkeep
5 Evaporative cooling and energy conservation
6 Treatment of surfaces, volumes, and enclosures in tropical city context
7 Tropical aesthetics in high-intensity urban context
8 Open building systems — building component development for adaptability and flexibility of use
9 Incremental construction — addition and adaptation
10 Enchantment — environmental aesthetics (ambience)
11 Role of idiosyncratic expression
12 Building typology and prototype reformation — type as social agreement
13 Community and privacy — urban conviviality and seclusion
14 Soft-edged building aesthetics
15 High ambient data levels — texture, grain, and activity information
16 Counter-cyclical building strategies
17 Automated households

The Aesthetic Agenda

1 Umbrella aesthetics — the section as generator rather than the enclosure
2 Integrating nature in buildings — seasonal variations
3 Aesthetics of shadow and shade rather than platonic volume and plane
4 Limits of cultural and ethnic symbolism — consensus, transformation, and innovation
5 Texture and scale correlated to activity and pace
6 Implied space and anticipatory psychology in form, space, and place
7 Human scale in dense settings
8 Cognition in high-intensity areas
9 Management of scale differences between intense developments and adjacent natural and heritage scales
10 Utilization of sound, smell, texture, theme, colour, and form in public places
11 Layering and matting of surfaces and spaces — interaction of groups and buildings
12 Profiles and silhouettes against overcast skies
13 Rhapsody in design and strategies for enchantment
14 Epistemology and pedagogy of form as a fundamentally inclusive design and artistic language system
15 The city as a collective work of art

The Social Agenda — A Civic Urban Culture

1 Passive participation

2 Active participation (structured)
3 Active participation (non-structured)
4 Active participation (non-anticipated)
5 Active participation (anticipated)
6 Active participation (by levels of participation)
7 A climate of public discourse — information culture — access and consequence
8 High information accessibility and open inquiry systems at different levels of entry — information navigation
9 Family locus in spatial arrangements — tri-nuclear households
10 Open autonomous research systems
11 Open economic systems with open information access
12 Interactive inquiry systems into social management mechanisms
13 Teleworking and proximity factors

The Interior Planning Agenda
1 Dwelling units for two family cycles — adaptability and seclusion
2 The tri-nuclear house — emotional place attachment and enhancement of family history and locality identification
3 Component design and internal adaptability
4 Veranda life-style
5 Tropical Asian kitchen
6 Humidity and storage
7 Ventilation and task air-conditioning
8 Psycho-physiological concepts

The Technological Windows

Contracted R&D and investment commitments:

1 Evaporative cooling technology — applied to whole city and each building
2 Energy modelling of whole city and each building
3 Micro climatic measurements and modelling of whole districts
4 Optimized cooling systems with sensing — intelligent hardware
5 Water use and recycling
6 Waste heat recovery in energy conservation
7 Desalination through use of waste heat
8 Vertical landscaping technology and plant type selection
9 Urban farming — hydroponics and hi-tech animal husbandry
10 Personal urban transport — electric vehicles and smart carts
11 Refuse processing and recycling
12 Solar energy for cooling and ventilation
13 Flash distillation
14 District cooling
15 Hyper-media for structured and non-structured communication and information access
16 Auto-reactive building utilities and building skins
17 Solar lighting for deep spaces
18 Energy storage
19 Building automation
20 Public place instant information systems
21 Low-labour building and city maintenance systems

22 Light-weight soils and rooting materials
23 Building components — open building system
24 Solar clothes dryers
25 Water-retentive surface materials for evaporative cooling
26 Rapid aerated packaged sewerage systems
27 Phototropic glass applications
28 Solar ventilation systems
29 Heat absorption cooling systems
30 Water repellant but breathing paints
31 Urban pest control systems
32 Remote control ventilation systems
33 Automated households
34 Photovoltaic building applications

Legal and Administrative Agenda

From the preceding statements I have made, I think it is very clear that we have a historic role to play in Singapore, and that is to develop a tropical city. This is also an international issue which relates to the global environment. The greenhouse effect is becoming a very big issue today. The Tropical City concept will contribute positively to that agenda. Then in a more concrete sense, we have the Strategic Planning Agenda, and that relates to the way in which we use land and building resources in Singapore. And directly under that is the Urban Design Agenda — how you actually put this thing together — this is the detailed Urban Design Agenda. Underneath that again in hierarchy is the Architectural Agenda.

Architecture would then have a proper framework in which to respond. Right now, the architectural agenda is actually dictated by architectural magazines and the glossy design and fashion picture books from overseas. Every time a new magazine comes out, it induces a new twist in our architectural design *ad nauseam*. Now underlining all these of course is the Aesthetic Agenda. And the Aesthetic Agenda is larger than the Architectural Agenda because it involves all the other arts as well. Then of course there is the Social Agenda. Earlier, I alluded to the issues arising from information culture. You cannot develop IT effectively if you are secretive. Basically, an information culture implies a more open access to information and use of IT implies some degree of transparency in information collection and dissemination. Relational data bases and interrogation systems need to be developed and given public access. Different attitudes towards information access, information control, information protection, and so on — it's a whole new area in itself. And it is culture-sensitive. Information inspection pulls in one direction, culture pulls in the other direction. Going right down the agenda list, there is the Interior Planning Agenda which affects the way our offices are planned, our homes are planned, our shopping centres are planned, the life-styles that go on inside, and so forth. I think the Product Agendas are more important to the Economic Development Board and Trade Development Board or Ministry of Trade and Industry. The Technological Windows are opened by the Intelligent Tropical City. The concept will focus issues and directions. Obviously, to implement the Intelligent Tropical City concept would involve investigating and developing new and also hybrid technologies, the parameters of which would be defined by environmental needs, and also defined by socio-economic parameters. Just to give you one example: air-conditioning in Singapore accounts for 50 per cent of the total national energy bill. That is an incredibly large amount that Singapore is spending. This fact is based on research done at the NUS (National University of Singapore). If only we can reduce the need for air-conditioning … I don't at all suggest that we can do away with it because I think air-conditioning is here to stay. That air-conditioning has a great deal of relevance in modern life cannot be denied. The question is how to create options for its use as well as how to reduce the energy required to produce comfort conditions. Then there are other issues like waste heat recovery in order to desalinate sea water, how to establish an urban ecological system so that the various technical systems as well as natural systems are ecologically balanced. It must all make economic sense in the end.

We can stop here now and go into the slides. Here we begin with some basic concepts and the most basic concept is that in the tropics it is uncomfortable to move about. Therefore, from the point of view of saving human energy as well as saving fuel energy costs, conservation of energy becomes the main issue and you can do this through compact multi-use planning. But it is not the mono-cultural compact planning as with current CBDs (central business districts). CBDs are basically only offices and banks, and this is built-in inefficiency because the infrastructure is used only half the time as at night most CBDs are completely dead. Moreover, CBDs exacerbate the journey-to-work dichotomy and time and energy is required to move people from their homes to the cities and vice versa. This is a problem we must overcome at source through planning. So in the tropical city, the basic idea is to integrate the various activities so that they are closely related to each other and the need to travel is reduced, and you can achieve certain synergies as a result of this. We will talk more about synergies later.

Some of the slides shown here are from a design workshop in October last year at the fourth year level at the NUS School of Architecture, which was conducted by Bob Powell, a few others at the School, and myself. The poor students were put through a three-week grind and we actually designed Marina South in three weeks! Basically it was to test extreme densities and whether it was possible to achieve the kind of mix we are talking about and whether the environment produced will be totally acceptable. If we could satisfy ourselves that it is liveable and that it has some coherence then we would have achieved at least one milestone, that is, to demonstrate that a compact, multi-use, high-density environment is viable. And here we were looking at a density of twelve-and-a-half times the land area. Just to give you a picture of this, the total floor space of parts of New York city is fifteen times the land area the buildings sit on. Downtown Hong Kong is similar, whereas in the Singapore situation the average floor space ratio is less than 3 for the downtown area when you take the total floor area divided by the total land area on which all the buildings sit. We are talking about moving up from 3 to somewhere around 12! The test here was to see whether it made sense. And I think the conclusion is that it does. I hope you also agree.

Now the other issue is the dwelling itself. Here we are talking about the space within the dwelling so that two family life cycles can take place within it. We thus conceive of a tri-nuclear household in which the three nuclei can connect or disconnect at will. The first nucleus is the work nucleus, the second nucleus is the first family nucleus, and the third nucleus is the second family nucleus. This concept was developed in my submission for the Kawasaki competition in 1986. The operating concept is connection *at will*. At present, a lot of interpersonal problems take place within the family space because there is no choice in spatial arrangements. What we want to do is to introduce choice into the spatial arrangements as well as introduce a workplace in the spatial arrangements. Some extent of teleworking will surely be needed. That is a subject in itself for more discussion and some investigation and perhaps some experimentation as well. How else can work take place in a family environment efficiently?

This is purely to show you that I am arguing for quite a determined intervention through city planning (Figure 1). There are of course those who argue that city planning must be a slow evolutionary process, and that heavy intervention by and large has produced rather unsatisfactory results in the past. I think that that particular view and that particular criticism of the heavy intervention approach is rather misinformed. That interventions in the past had been unsatisfactory does not in itself invalidate intervention as such. We can discuss that a bit more because one needs to look into the history of intervention. Many heads are needed but there must be consensus of the overall concept and aims to be achieved. If there is consensus no heavy-handedness will result.

Figure 1: Massive intervention must mean many initiatives by architects and developers. The Tropical City concept is a collective form of many smaller parts (model by NUS fourth-year students at a workshop on Intelligent Tropical City, October 1988).

The concept of the Intelligent Tropical City is really that of a very large shophouse where you live upstairs and work downstairs (Figure 2). We are talking about large covered outdoor areas for outdoor activities with shelter from the rain and sun spanning between buildings. We are also talking about bridging structures between buildings so that you can move from one building to another without having to go down to the ground if you so choose. We are also talking about roof-tops being connected throughout the city. So, in effect we create two grounds, one on the earth and one in the podium roof-tops. And we are also talking about landscaping the roof-tops and introducing community and recreational facilities at the upper levels — features which at the moment are not at all considered in any of the cities in the tropics.

In the study done at the NUS School of Architecture, the issue as to why concentrate on Marina South was discussed as a strategic planning issue. The present population of Singapore is 2.6 million and projections are that it would level off at around 3.2 million in 2015. But as you know projections can be quite far off. So let's say about a million people have to be catered for in the next twenty to thirty years. And where would we put them? Obviously, there are several options. One option, which is the customary option, is to build new towns at the perimeters. The industrial estates and new towns are the result of this strategy. And that has been the new pattern in the last twenty-five years. So we examined the possibility and implications of putting half a million people in the downtown area. And indeed the moment we pose that question, we free the pressure on the surrounding unbuilt, natural, and historic areas a lot more than at present.

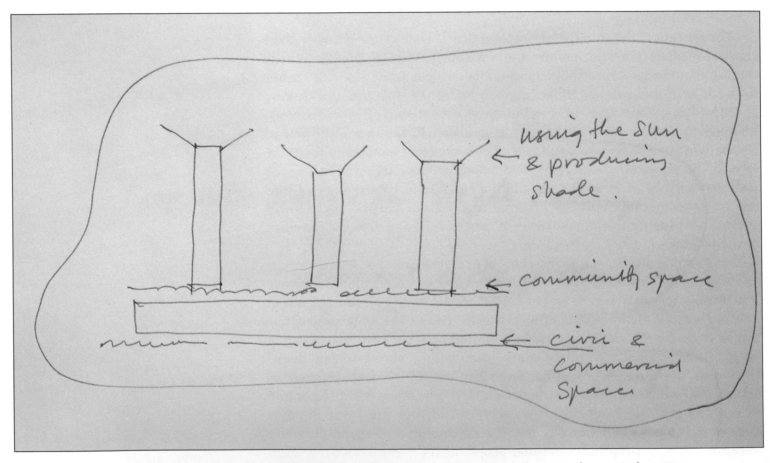

Figure 2: The basic morphology of the tropical city is the creation of an upper level community connective space over the traditional ground floor commercial space.

And I am very glad to read the Minister's recent speech indicating that a review is taking place. Now the other implication of the increase in the downtown population density is the impact on the MRT (Mass Rapid Transit) system. Obviously the MRT system will have to be extended further if you build more new towns outside and that means incurring higher costs as well as carrying the financial burden of underutilized trains during non-peak hours. This must obviously be a serious economic burden on the MRT system. However, if the downtown population is greatly increased, then the utilization of trains going out of the city during peak hours will increase and so will non-peak hour usage, especially if the schools are outside the central area. So we are talking about a synergistic relationship between downtown population size and the transport system for the good of both.

In computing the desirable density for the downtown area of which the Marina sites are a part, the methodology was to compute the estimated per capita floor space that Singaporeans presently occupy — residential, workplace, markets, retail, recreation, education, culture, utility, hotels, and so on — this works to approximately 53 sq. metres per person. Based on 53 sq. metres per person times the population and divided by the land area in Marina South, which is 540 hectares, we arrive at a gross plot ratio of 5. And since we are not going to build over the entire land — we can't because we have roads and parks and stuff like that — we are talking about building on 40 per cent of the land. Therefore, the gross plot ratio becomes a net of 12.5. So that becomes our target density because without being thus computed, the Urban Design and Architectural Agendas have no basis. Too many urban design concepts have neglected this basic computation and therefore are not able to address real issues. Reactions to this density are basically negative because the existing precedents are not good. Low density too has indeed become a doctrine of the so-called humanists. And this doctrine is deeply embedded in the consciousness of most town planners. The real issue is how to deploy floor space in a manner conducive to convenience and comfort. That is the real challenge. Studies of basic generic building forms have to be undertaken. We tried out various models. And the preferred model is the one in Figure 3, which is a basket weave of building blocks which allow a flow of air through from different directions and which also produce the required floor space. We always have to test that our designs can actually produce the needed space and also produce the environment that is liveable and desirable. So that is how we came to the conclusion that a net density of 12.5 is viable. Conceptually, it is as in Figure 2, with the tower blocks at the top, the community space at the roof-top of the podium block, and the civic and commercial space on the ground floor. This separation is deliberate; it uses the roof space as a space resource, which at the moment in most buildings is not used. Mind you this form is quite common really. And there are many buildings in Singapore like this. If you look at the Shenton Way buildings, they are like this but unfortunately all the roof-tops are just concrete decks for machinery. Look at Bras Brasah Complex, look at Upper Cross Street Complex, look at Waterloo Centre and People's Park Complex. They all have this form but the roof decks are not used. The roof decks are concrete and they are heat traps, and they suffer from lack of facilities. Their use must be part of the

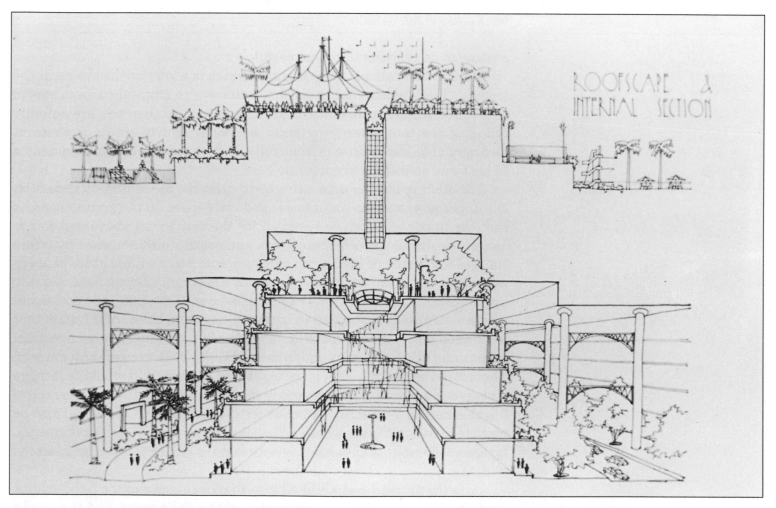

ROOFSCAPE &
INTERNAL SECTION

Figure 3: Planting and landscaping of roofs is a vital part of the urban environment strategy.

routine of daily living to be successful.

We will now talk about heat traps, which is a very critical issue in the tropics. The fundamental environmental issue in tropical cities is how to reduce the temperature of the whole city. Because then you are actually reducing the total energy required to cool it and to create a pleasant environment. The roof decks when fully landscaped will be a good insulator of heat and so will not accumulate heat.

The other reason for separating the two levels, the community space on the upper level and the commercial and civic space on the ground level, is that the upper level can be reserved for the residences above and this is socially desirable for neighbourliness and social cohesion. And therefore the roof-top should be used as a means to accommodate those kinds of needs as well as to foster the development of community spirit, whereas the ground floor is more the universal, impersonal, civic space, the social and economic transactional space which every city must have. And I think that here anonymity is a good thing. People should be able to escape from community into anonymity and from anonymity back to community at will. There must be choice — that is the essence of city living. It would be terrible if everyday we have to see everybody that we know. That too is the kind of life that can be a tyranny. So much for the village idyll. It would also be terrible to live in a place where nobody knows anybody. And that also is a tyranny. We want to have a mix of both and the choice to move between the two.

So in the particular study at NUS — the first stage was the fixed volume study which was purely an evaluation of the floor space and the blocks

without considering the aesthetics or environmental or micro climate or micro environmental factors. In the second stage we began to develop some kind of civic sense, some kind of cognitive location planning, some idea of movement pattern, that is, how people can move from one place to another, how to separate between service vehicles, pedestrian traffic, and so on and so forth (Figure 4). This is a beginning in the response to the human factor in dense city planning but this is all very preliminary, all that was possible to do during a three-week programme. I would suggest that this project itself be a springboard for further research and further design. This is just the beginning of the Urban Design Agenda. If you look at Figure 5, you can see that there is quite a lot of open space. Though it is quite busy I think you agree with me that it is not unliveable. A lot can be done to the design to make it better and more liveable and cognitively clearer, but these are very detailed considerations. When you look closer, you see that this kind of pattern — I would like to contrast it with the New York pattern which is a great grid iron — actually promotes total anonymity. What we want is a pattern in which the choice between anonymity and community is available. In New York you have no choice. Whatever community there is takes place indoors in class-defined enclaves. And that leads to the kind of social problems of New York. Figure 6 is a proposal for the ground floor, which could look something like this with a weave of spaces that go between buildings. There should be clarity and a lot of pedestrian space between buildings because traffic can be routed to the perimeter, and vehicles are allowed in only during restricted hours.

Figure 7 would be a personal rapid transit system that runs on the roof-

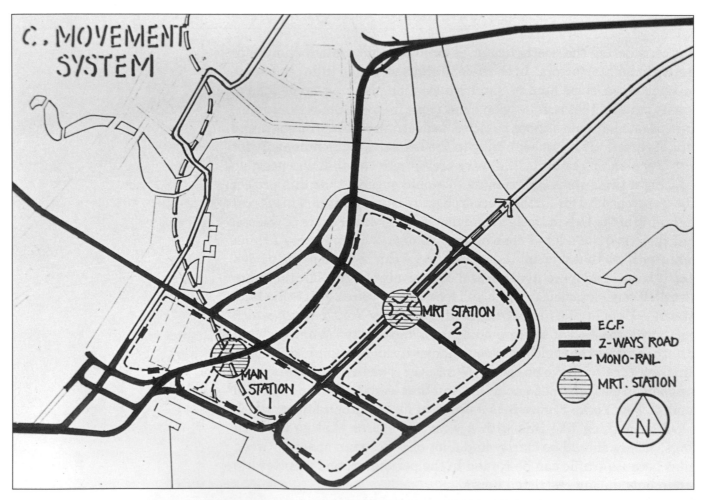

Figure 4: All cars are routed to the perimeter of the pedestrianized zones, which are served by a Personalized Rapid Transport system.

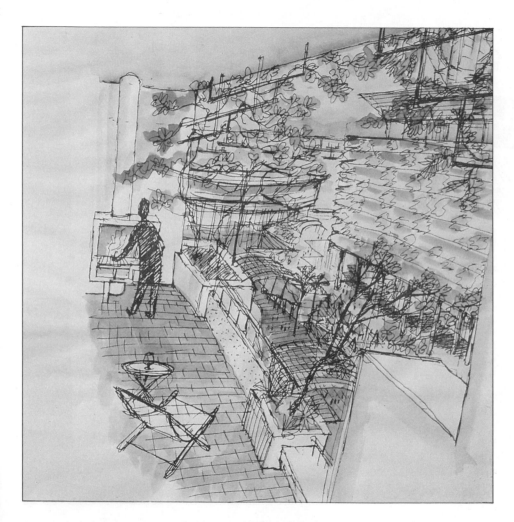

Figure 5: Open living on balconies is possible only when the whole urban micro climate is conducive. Reduced temperature, more wind movement, low noise, and less dust is the aim of the Tropical City concept.

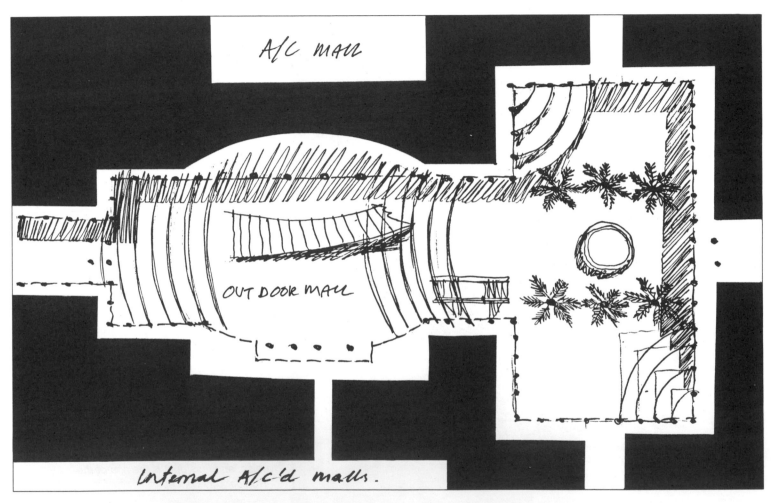

A/C mall

OUTDOOR MALL

Internal A/c'd malls.

Figure 6: Typical ground floor plan with civic facilities and covered outdoor spaces.

Figure 7: Electric levitation train running on roof-tops for personal transit.

tops. In this particular proposal, we looked at the possibility of incorporating a magnetic levitation train — the type being implemented in Las Vegas. It is very silent and apparently quite economical — that is the kind of system we could have. You could imagine these buildings in Figure 8 as community centres, with swimming pools on the roof-tops; clubs, churches, mosques, restaurants, all arranged for mutual support on the roof-tops. So we are talking about creating a kind of *kampung* on the roof-tops — an urban community. An alternative road transport system we are thinking of is that of a small electric vehicle which carries four persons (Figure 9). It could be computer-controlled and circulate through the city; it could branch off, and then merge back onto special guideways. There can be flexibility in the tracking. And there are many other systems to be investigated, each of them with its own characteristics and price tag. If Singapore were to adopt such a system, I think we could have a negotiating position even of buying into the patent. I think that if the contract is large enough, the negotiating position can be good. This is the kind of possibility that I think we should look into. I think the building of the tropical city would also involve products which we could develop by ourselves too. Singapore hasn't yet got that kind of scope, but with bold foresight this should be possible. And we could make arrangements with producers and manufacturers to our advantage for downstream marketing. Because of our showcase position we can enhance the export of some of these new products. Such transport systems should be running around the edges of each building precinct. Each of these environmental areas was determined by a 10-minute walk from the centre to the edge. So, within each of these

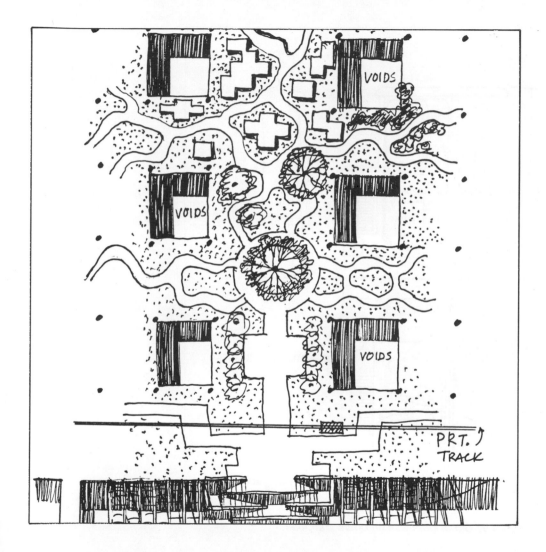

Figure 8: Podium roof plan.

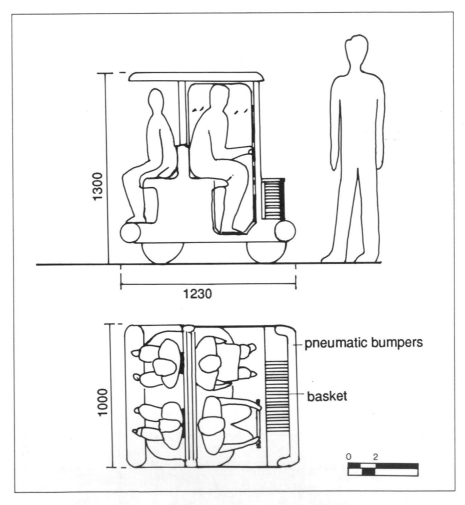

1300

1230

1000

pneumatic bumpers

basket

0   2

Figure 9: Smart carts with on-board computer.

environmental areas we are talking about a high degree of pedestrianization. But there will also be vehicles such as the shopping-cart, battery-operated vehicle, or this kind of vehicle which could have an on-board computer (Figure 10) for it to function as an automatic taxi. You just press a button and it will go to your destination. And it will have automatic accident-avoidance systems with pneumatic bumpers. Somebody is already developing something like this for materials handling in Singapore. I think it's only a small step to go from there to a "smart cart" system like this. And again all these are products based on existing technologies. In fact, the technological developments that we have cited in the Technological Windows are all adaptive and applications technologies. We are not talking about any really new technologies. All we have to do is to adapt and hybridize. There are therefore spin-offs related to the Intelligent Tropical City concept.

I would now like to summarize. Earlier, I talked about synergies. I talked about not just a mono-cultural CBD, not just housing or offices but a rich urban mix; I talked about mixing CBD functions and housing. I am also talking about urban universities. We conceptualized a third university to be down in the city. But it could very well be an offshore campus for other universities, even from elsewhere. NUS too could have a downtown portion of its campus for, say, business administration, economics, or banking studies. This could be located in town to benefit from specific locational factors. The new Design School may also be part of the city; NTI (Nanyang Technological Institute) engineering, say urban environmental engineering, could be in the city as well. And we might also be thinking of bringing

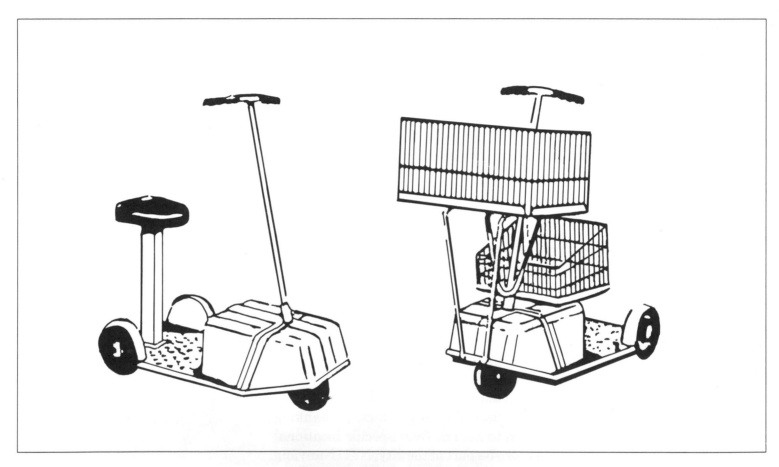

Figure 10: Electric shopping-carts.

in foreign universities to establish post-graduate research programmes here too. And I don't see why we should not build into the city itself the mix between business and academia. For example, the vigour in the high-tech industries in Cambridge, Massachusetts arises precisely because of the close relationship between the academic and business environments as professors move back and forth between the business and research environments. And this is the kind of positive interaction we want to foster. This is intelligent planning. A very important study done by Everett Rogers on the Silicon Valley attests to the fact that brainstorming sessions that take place outside the company are as productive as those within. These take place between creative people from different companies in the restaurants and lounges along the main spine of Silicon Valley — that's where the great ideas come from. Proximity and intimacy are important factors. I know it's often been argued that Singapore is so small that distances are not great and therefore there is no need for proximity. But it's amazing how far it can be — when people are out of sight, they are out of mind! And I also think that telecommunications as a medium of interaction is good only for specific and structured communication. Non-specific and non-structured interaction does not often take place on the electronic media because people don't ring up and say "Hey! I really have nothing to say, but just want to chat with you". People just don't do that in the workday. Leisurely conversations often turn up new ideas just by chance. Serendipity is an important part of urban culture, but it is usually neglected in urban planning. The purpose of cities after all is to facilitate transactions. Today the shift is towards the transaction of ideas. Thank you.

DISCUSSION

CHAIRMAN

The discussion is now open to the floor. As we deliberate on possibilities, we may want to bear in mind that the laws and concepts governing urban planning, land-use, patterns of housing, open spaces, and so on, in Southeast Asia are to a considerable degree still based on models derived from Britain, France, Holland, and the United States. True adaptations and modifications have occurred, but have these been sufficient? Is a massive overhaul imperative?

QUESTION

Can I follow up on that and ask whether the city you have outlined, Tay Kheng Soon, can only be built by a centralized authority?

TAY KHENG SOON

The basic premiss of all the studies done so far has been to provide for incrementality and that means sectional and phased implementation. It also implies multiple-agency interventions. I am not advocating, at all, a single-agency approach. I think the single-agency approach has been the main culprit in the dissatisfaction with the massive intervention approach. All the grand plans like the building of Brazilia in the 50s and in the 60s are imposed by a single vision of the city. And of course they are quite sterile — they don't work. Ironically, in Brazilia the really active section is the adjacent squatter settlement. That's where the real action is. That's where all the multiple initiatives take place and that explains its vibrancy. So not only is the life of a place affected by the single-agency massive intervention approach, but the capital involved would be unman-ageable. A lively city has to be implemented in parts, but there must be an overall concept and linkages must be planned for. The infrastructure has to be laid out. The land should be parcelled out for separate builders and architects. And individual builders and developers can come in, but there must be controls — roof-tops must link up; floors must link. Right now, the laws work against the use and the linking up of roof-tops. So I think it is a matter of changing one section of the law at a time. I am not talking about a total overhaul of the legal system — that is out of the question. In keeping with the incremental approach, we are talking about modifications to the existing legal structure, to allow for easements and rights of way and clarification of obligations so as to create a unified city rather than a fragmented one. And there are lots of legal precedents for easements between property owners to draw from. But administrators tend not to like these things because they are messy — because every bridge between one building and another implies an agreement that must survive over time, does it not? You cannot have a bridge with only one support; you need both sides. What happens if one side decides to demolish his building? Is he constrained not to demolish his building? The legal issues could be messy. But there are many precedents to sort them out. I think the main fear that we are talking about is the fear of the dominance of the one big idea to be implemented by one central authority at one time. This of course is not at all the intention of what I am proposing. In any case it would be unrealistic.

A project has to be phased and implemented over time. Specifically in the Singapore context, nothing speaks more eloquently than a real demonstration project. We should identify a project of manageable size to focus on and to design in the new ideas — the legal, the physical, and the investment agendas for a particular site. The best site is at Kampong Bugis (Figure 11). It has the best chance of success because it could be the most desirable urban housing site there is in the whole of Southeast Asia! At the moment the URA's (Urban Redevelopment Authority) concept plan is for some low-rise blocks and one high-rise block. The site has tremendous development potentials. It is a very good site because it is so close to the city. It is also surrounded by, and facing, water on three sides: it's superb. Two MRT stations serve the site. All the infrastructure is there too. It's ready. This is the site to build the first Intelligent Tropical City. And the next step should be Marina South and Marina East. At Kampong Bugis we are talking about maybe 50,000 people being housed and working in the scheme. By building in phases we would iron out all the bugs and all the problems. So I would say straightaway, stop building into the outer areas of the island. Maintain maximum options for the outer areas of the island. Concentrate on the inner urban area. Don't destroy what's left of the countryside.

QUESTION

I am not an architect. I am from the engineering profession. I felt that what you said — how it be best pursued — has already been pursued by the space scientists. When you are in space, you don't have the earth and other connections and other requirements — you're self-contained, self-

Figure 11: Kampong Bugis is an ideal site for testing the dense Tropical City concept. This proposal by the Urban Redevelopment Authority (URA) underutilizes the land.

supporting, and all that. So why couldn't we use these technologies for the tropical city?

TAY KHENG SOON

I don't think we need so much high-tech. That's why I said that the technologies actually needed in the Intelligent Tropical City are not new ones. The Tropical City concept should not mean having to reinvent the wheel. There are lots of environmental control technologies which already exist in various forms. Space research has produced some of the systems. But I am not too happy about space systems because they are all very expensive. There are other systems, for example, very simple things like photovoltaics, say, to light deep spaces, which we need. Because if you are building at this kind of density, at the lower levels — the spaces can be quite broad, maybe 100 feet wide — sunlight is not going to penetrate right into the centre of such spaces. Now it is a very simple thing to bring the sunlight into the centre because there is a new product which is being developed by an Australian group. It is a flexible acrylic rod which can transmit sunlight right through to the interior of buildings and costs only S$10 a metre in length — it's very cheap. At present it is used only for decorative lighting. This could be a product which could be further developed in Singapore. It's actually applications technology rather than fundamental research that we need. Now, another technology that exists is photo-chromatic glass (Figure 12) — glass that can adjust its opacity depending on temperature and intensity of light. So when we are talking about large covered areas, photo-chromatic glass is available. There are also other

*Figure 12: Covered outdoor space —
Serangoon Club, Singapore.*

kinds of photo-tropic glass operating through a small electrical charge. Just flick a switch and the whole thing goes opaque. You can think of windows where with the flick of a switch they go black. So you can cut down unwanted light and so on. These are very simple things — they already exist. And in the field of photovoltaic developments, for example, things are moving fast. We are now talking about 13 to 14 per cent efficiency. Whereas in the past, photovoltaics produced only 10 to 11 per cent efficiency, advanced models are going up to 35 per cent efficiency. So, it's possible to think of the roof-tops as a photovoltaic energy source powering the city without pollution. These are just adaptations and applications. They are not new things at all. As they come into the market, they can be applied.

QUESTION

I'm concerned that concentrating the population would pose a defence problem. Wouldn't scattering the population be better?

TAY KHENG SOON

Well, the best defence for Singapore is to make friends. I think that building a wall is no defence for a small island city-state. But all I can say is that in any kind of population concentration — whether HDB estate or the Intelligent Tropical City — there is no difference in terms of the kind of risk, if it comes to that.

CHAIRMAN

Defence can be designed afterwards. . . .

TAY KHENG SOON

I think of defence in terms of making friends and in terms of being useful to others. Right now, the economies of the tropical cities, as I said earlier, are merely production bases and import-substituting bases. Therefore, they are primarily in conflict with each other because they are competing for the same markets and the same investors. Now, if we add a new sector which produces products which benefit others in the tropics and our neighbours, won't this, at least to some extent, moderate the essentially conflictual situation? Indeed, I can see, for example, the Intelligent Tropical City concept leading to economic complementation in ASEAN, as development of new technologies and their applications could generate new areas of co-operative enterprise for ASEAN as a whole.

QUESTION

What are the sociological implications of the Intelligent Tropical City particularly with respect to family life?

TAY KHENG SOON

I think the problem of families is a very serious one; it has long-range implications and short-range implications, what with mothers working and children being brought up by Filipino maids as in many middle-class families in Singapore today. It's obviously not the best solution. I think some kind of accommodation between the desire to work and the desire to participate in the economy of the country and the self-satisfaction that derives from that cannot be denied our women. At the moment it's being traded off against proper family life and children take the brunt of it all. That trade-off is tearing at the family unit. And the cost of society reproducing itself is mounting. I think this is a real and difficult issue. I don't see why, for example, a secretary can't work at home via teleworking technology. I don't see why in my profession, for example, I need to go to the office except for meetings with staff and to meet clients and things like that. I can easily work from home if I have the tele-linkages. A lot of thinking work can be done at home if we have hyper-media or any of the broad-band information systems which allow for efficient data transfers and visual communications. Actually, video phones and such-like devices would make it quite viable. I think the answer to your question is that the micro-sociological context of the family has to be considered. And distance is an issue. Even if it means leaving for a few minutes to go shopping, a terrible catastrophe can happen to a child left alone at home. I think anybody who has brought up young children would know it can be very worrying. Then of course the other issue is the aged, and society is ageing fast. There are also tasks which those in their sixties and seventies can still do in the workplace environment but at the moment it's difficult to do so because the division of household duties and spatial arrangements make it difficult. Compact planning and teleworking can solve to some extent these problems and open up new working life-styles.

QUESTION
Would it be possible to have workplaces nearer where people live?

TAY KHENG SOON

I have to tell you that right now the laws work against this possibility, and for not very good reasons. I posed this question at a dialogue with the Ministry of National Development. I posed the hypothetical situation of putting an office building in Serangoon Gardens Estate. The immediate reaction was that of horror. My argument was that there may be some companies that want to be located at that place precisely because they want to tap the part-time female labour force. And the part-time female labour force would prefer to work in offices nearby too. But the laws, that is, the town planning regulations and land-use classifications, the licensing rules — all work against it. For example, if you want to put a telex machine at home, you must first have a downtown business address before you are permitted to fix a telex machine at your house. It's absurd. This problem arises because it is tied into development charges, which is a tax-collection device. So the issue gets tangled with the whole administrative tax-collecting mechanism. With the proper perspective, review, and a new vision, we can untangle it and make a more rational mix of uses possible and desirable.

CHAIRMAN

What you are suggesting has a basic problem. If I were an administrator, I could view your suggestion as a certain kind of disorder being injected into a system which is ordered. So, how are you going to sell it? After all, enormous amounts of money and energy have gone into trying to fashion a system that has a certain degree of order, a certain degree of control, a certain degree of economic efficiency. In other words, to sell your idea, you will have to demonstrate that what you are proposing is going to be just as ordered, just as economic, and in no way destructive to all the existing plans. Furthermore, that its incorporation will produce a better life for Singaporeans.

TAY KHENG SOON
I have said that we have to have an experimental phase where ideas are developed in some depth before they can be fitted into the existing systems.

CHAIRMAN
The experimental project in Kampong Bugis would have to virtually guarantee the people who are going to move to that particular area in perhaps a hermetically sealed fashion, that they can work there, live there, and that there would be follow-up research on life there. In a way it could be a controlled experiment.

TAY KHENG SOON
I don't think the Tropical City concept is something that's hermetically sealed. It's got to be a permeable space system. It's part of the total spacial system. People must be able to come and go. Choice must be there, too.

CHAIRMAN
Let me clarify. What I am saying is that your experiment might result in the development of a system which would be perfectly workable for the

area because you are going to design it as such. But the moment your society moves into the outer environment, the hinterland, it will be operating differently. The question then would be whether there would be too much contrast as to make your experiment not easily transferable to other places.

TAY KHENG SOON

But we have many such areas already. There are many areas that have characteristics which are unique. Like private housing estates, like the HDB housing estates, like the industrial towns, like the Orchard Road area — these all have characteristics of their own, an internal logic of their own. But in no way does it really contradict or impose unbearable strains on other sections — provided there is a legal framework that rules over the disparities. And we do have these systems here. In other cities where control is weak, then our proposal may act as a fuse to detonate the tenuous social balance that exists. But I think in the Singapore case, you do not have this problem because there is a very powerful, very strong supervening administrative structure. It can override the disparities. This issue was discussed during a workshop at the National University of Singapore in 1988. There was a concern that the Intelligent Tropical City should not become a social enclave. Will it be separate from the rest of the island? What kind of people are going to live there? Are they going to be just a very privileged class of people? The answer is no. Because they should be a cross-section of Singaporeans, which market forces will eventually decide. The spatial allocations will be different of course. And therefore, the opportunities for different kinds of life-styles will exist for all its inhabitants.

QUESTION
In your Technological Windows, it's important to identify what are the critical technologies that must take place before a tropical city like this can happen, and then concentrate on how the tropical city can adapt over time without changing everything overnight. A city is not a one-shot affair.

TAY KHENG SOON
There are various gadgets and technologies and everybody has pet ideas. I too have my own preferences. Ultimately all ideas have to be tested by the market. Will the market really buy it? You may have some fantastic idea but if nobody wants it, then it's not on. For example, the question of energy saving for air-conditioning can be a very important issue. Dr S.P. Rao of the Building Science Department at the National University of Singapore (NUS) has shown some remarkable findings. He did a controlled experiment with two standardized rooms: one room normal, and the other one, he sprayed with water on the outside. The total energy required to cool the one with the water spray required 25 per cent less energy to cool than the normal room. This indicates that evaporative cooling may be an important technology. We should be looking into *evaporative cooling* of buildings in open public places as well: the cooling of public space around a group of buildings is indicated. Some of the ideas developed during the NUS workshop explored spraying a mist of water

on buildings so that plants can grow and thus also cool the building in the process (Figure 13). And if you want air-conditioning, then your air-conditioning bill could also be 25 per cent less! Now, the maintenance bill question. I know that the monthly maintenance bill for vertical landscaping of one of Singapore's leading hotels is approximately S$30,000. That's a lot (Figure 14). And that could be because the planting system has not been optimized. That's not surprising as there has been virtually no R&D on vertical landscaping. Vertical landscaping is therefore an important R&D subject to be studied in terms of upstream to downstream effects — what kinds of plants, the appropriate rooting materials, pest control, plant growth systems — these are all research topics in themselves. When the technology is mature and more widespread then prices will be more competitive.

QUESTION

Does research therefore need to develop a new range of materials which can be sprayed with water, which can give up water at the same time by evaporation and yet not deteriorate with bacteria and fungi?

TAY KHENG SOON

No, not everything is new. Only some new things are needed. In fact, the old clay roof tiles did precisely that because they were partially absorbent. They retained water and on hot days released the water through evaporation. This kept roofs cool. Now, we could consider that kind of material for wall surfaces too. But it means a different aesthetics. It means

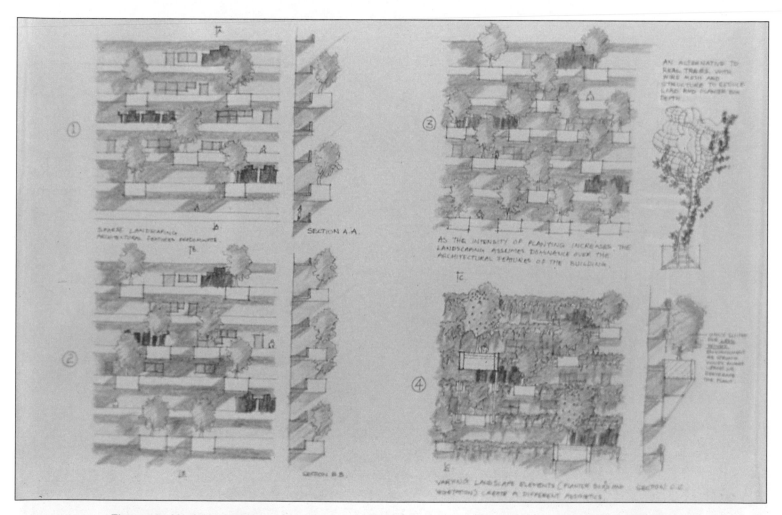

Figure 13: Vertical landscaping to soften the environment and to provide shade and evaporative cooling.

Figure 14: An example of successful vertical landscaping.

architects really have to put on their thinking caps and not just copy from magazines all the time. How we design single buildings and groups of buildings in the tropics to produce a cooling of the spaces in and around them is the real challenge. Aesthetic prejudices have no place in the search for new solutions. A new aesthetic has to be sought. No old ones are good enough.

CHAIRMAN

Well, perhaps we should study structures like Borobudur. The inside of such structures is very cool in the day and yet warm at night. And their builders didn't go to London!

TAY KHENG SOON

The kind of research that we have to do should be valid all over the tropical world. There is a unique study by Dr Sham Sani from the University of Malaya, Geography Department. The study is extremely interesting. It was funded by Unesco. Dr Sham Shani took temperatures along a transect from Port Kelang to Kuala Lumpur. The blobs in Figure 15 show the heat islands and they correspond to the highly urbanized areas. The temperatures in the centres of the heat islands on that particular day of 14 May 1986 averaged between 34 and 36 °C, whereas outside in the open field the ambient temperature was approximately 31 °C. So there was a 4 °C increase of temperature because of the heat island effect in the city centres. And he went on to discuss the formation of heat islands (Figure 16) — noting the "canyon effect" as buildings trap the air, trap the heat, and the

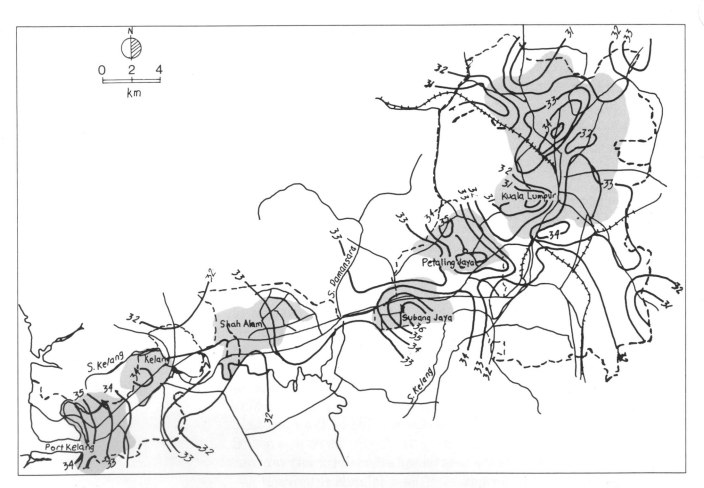

Figure 15: Distribution of afternoon temperatures in the Kelang Valley, 14 May 1986.

Figure 16: Heavily built-up areas produce the "heat island and heat canyon" effects.
Night-time temperatures remain high due to heat island effect.

heat re-radiates within the space which then builds up. The opposite of the heavy built-up environment is the tropical rain forest (Figure 17). Typically, the tropical rain forest is 4 to 5 °C lower in temperature than the ambient temperature in an open field situation. If you take the temperature in an open football field and compare it with the temperature in a tropical rain forest, it's between 4 and 5 °C lower in the forest. So, we have a tremendous contrast. We are talking about between 8 and 10° C difference between the urban centre and the tropical rain forest. That to me is a strong suggestion for shading and evaporative cooling to be part of a Tropical Urban Design Agenda. How we merge these two environments is the design problem. If you can merge these two environments then we can settle for somewhere around a four or five degree reduction in the city area — that is the critical area for climatic and design research.

CHAIRMAN

Agree. Even now, here, whenever there is rain outside, the temperature inside drops. The variation could be five to ten degrees. More importantly, how are you going to sell your planning ideas across the region because of entrenched laws and conflicting interests? In Singapore, you might be able to do it. Why? Because we are rebuilding the whole city. The government owns some 75 per cent of the land. And therefore, it's easier to legislate. But, say, in Kuala Lumpur they can't even get a road through to the old Batu Road area because of the cumbersome compensation system that is still operating there. How are you going to modify the laws governing planning?

Figure 17: The cool tropical forest — cooled by transpiration and shade.

TAY KHENG SOON

Development control is one of the major hurdles any new planning or architectural concept has to cross. Because development control rules are designed precisely to standardize the environmental design response. Because the role of development control is to protect the third party, you see. That third party could be the public user or the neighbour. The control is precisely for that and that is why you cannot build beyond the road because you have to respect the third party who may drive along in a truck that stands twenty feet high and bash up your porch. Third-party rights and individual obligations need to be re-defined.

CHAIRMAN

Is the tropical city going to create problems, say, with regard to mobilization of constituents?

TAY KHENG SOON

I think that if you have a lot of social interaction and if you connect the community system to the housing and workplace systems, you have an integration between the two, both physically as well as functionally. Then, to that extent, you are devolving some political control, which from the point of view of the control authority, would seem to be a loss of control. So, this could be a dilemma. If you want to have an environment in which the civic and cultural life of the people are much more convivial and conducive to community development, you may have to allow more initiative. I suppose in Singapore, the issue would be the extent of devolution and under what terms — that's a question I can't answer. I think it's an important question though. But I can see the outline of it — that there will be more such issues as we move forward. Psychological defence is involved too. And on this I could argue another way, that the extent to which people develop a rootedness and a sense of commitment to a place, to that extent they would defend it. If they have no sense of rootedness, no sense of identity, they would not defend it. Or they may defend it if they have no choice. But if they have a choice, they will run. Participation, I think, is essential to rootedness.

CHAIRMAN

I thought one of the great attractions of a Malay house or a *kampung* is that in them culture is not against but in harmony with the environment — the heat, the water, and all that. The environment is regarded as an asset and people enjoy it. In other words, you don't start getting really upset if you get wet, or if the sun is too hot, and so on. So you are going to design a place which now takes into account the assets of heat and water as positive forces. How are you going to try to integrate these into and with very tall buildings?

TAY KHENG SOON

Firstly, the whole idea must make economic sense to people who live there. It must also feel good to live in the Intelligent Tropical City — with regard to aesthetics as well as physical comfort and it must be convenient. So, all the plus points must be there. If they're not there, and with the general negative experience people have of living in cities it will be difficult. The usual view of most Westernized people is that the city is not a nice place to live in. It will take great ingenuity and design flair to change this. But price and convenience are powerful factors in people's preferences, too. Styling and good ambience must be provided.

CHAIRMAN

Let's take even this campus here. On a Western campus, in North America for instance, students, staff, everybody walks — even miles. Walking 500 yards between one lecture and another is nothing rare. This is virtually impossible here, because people get drenched in sweat walking such distances under the blazing sun. So, the question really is how do you do it so that our people will walk.

TAY KHENG SOON

The city is, as shown by Dr Sham Sani, 4 to 5 °C hotter than the surrounding environment. So, to start with, it's uncomfortable. And then, on top of that, the physical distance to walk — the climbing up and down the steps and all that is a big hassle. That's why the physical design must be very carefully considered in the tropics. It has to be convenient. People should not have to move a lot. And if they need to move a lot, there must be convenient means of transport. The environment must not be noisy and dusty and too crowded. And you have to have your landscaping and evaporative cooling and high-level shading and so forth. You must shade the buildings.

You can even have fans that drive wind through public spaces during the 50 per cent of the time in the tropics when there is no wind. We are talking about giant fans driving wind through city spaces and these propellers can be driven by turbines from the rain-water stored on the roof-tops. It is essential that unless you can create an environment that's really demonstratively better than the cities people are used to, the concept is not on. Why should anyone live in a tropical city just because it is labelled as such? It's got to be significantly better. And to make it better calls for research, creative thinking, and putting your thinking caps on.

QUESTION

What you are proposing is stimulating, especially because we are still using outmoded town planning concepts of Eberneezer Howard and those of Sir Patrick Abercrombie, developed in his plan for London, and enunciated as long ago as 1952. Since then there have been few new ideas. And as such your proposals for an Intelligent Tropical City are most interesting. Having said this, however, would they be accepted by the decision makers? For instance, I wonder whether Eberneezer Howard's garden city concept would have been accepted were it not based on the political framework and the political ideas of the time. Today is another such moment — we read of the depletion of the ozone layer and the need to do something about polluting energy resources. We also read about the depletion of the rain forests in this part of the world. It seems to me that the political climate might be just about right to accepting a new tropical planning paradigm. What do you think?

TAY KHENG SOON

Obviously you cannot find a cure for every kind of problem. The proposition of course is to conceptualize new kinds of dense urban centres. That aspect — that is, intensification — I think is applicable in other cases as well because of the damaging horizontal spread of cities which creates tremendous problems. In fact, right now I am looking at a particular city in the ASEAN region where we are making a proposal for one section of it to be developed along the lines that we have discussed, but strangely, for a different set of reasons. The fact about cities in the tropical world is that there is gross income disparity and gross disparity in opportunities. Too much wealth is also concentrated in the hands of a few people. The tactic is therefore how to use such wealth to create a better infrastructure for the city as a spin-off. There is a symbiosis between those who are wealthy and those who are not, though they may have different interests. They require each other because nobody really wants a revolution if they can help it. So, there has to be a consensus and it's possible to use spin-offs from dense developments, which also have other impacts, in terms of mobilizing capital, in terms of downstream flows into the poorer sections of the economy. The trickle-down effect can be accelerated — provided you can build up a climate of confidence. These are all very location-specific. Right now, I have no time to discuss the idea of balanced rural and urban developments. But it's not enough to consider a city in itself — the rural to urban drift needs rural centres to be developed as counter magnets. In Malaysia, for example, we have actually had some discussions about our concept of Production Towns being built in the countryside. As you know, the countryside is losing population. Population has been drifting to the urban centres. The plantations are undermanned — not enough rubber tappers so there are nearly 300,000 illegal immigrants from Indonesia to the plantations. They will obviously have to introduce higher-yield methods of plantation management and control. For example, rice cultivation is an area in which mechanization could have a major production impact. But it's moving at a slow pace and there are social and cultural costs too. We are talking about regrouping rural populations into production towns of about 30,000–40,000 people built around agro industries. These can then support reasonably good quality schools, hospitals, other amenities which at the moment are just so dispersed that they cannot function well. Typically, a school in the Malaysian countryside context would be a two-classroom school. And teachers have to be dragged by the hair to go and teach in those schools. Everbody wants to get out as soon as possible! So, you have problems. The kind of rural poverty/ignorance cycle gets reinforced by the physical settlement pattern. So, the concept is not just cities. We are talking about urbanizing the countryside and ruralizing the cities. To some extent, I think, in Malaysia they are beginning to look at this. I think Korean companies have come in to discuss the setting up of some kind of a township in the plantation areas. And then, of course, link up such townships for manufacturing industries, especially those related to wood products which are needed for urban centres' doors and windows and these can be made in the production towns. Right now in Singapore, for example, we can't even buy a proper door and window because every door and window has to be made on-site. There is no proper component industry.

Why is it not possible to have a whole range of factories in Johor Bahru in the plantations to supply to Singapore? These are areas in which economic complementation in a concrete sense is possible. It's a very complex issue — parts of it may be replicable, parts of it not. But I think there is also the importance of demonstration effects. If you can demonstrate success, then the chance of selling it to somebody else is better. The point which I wish to make is that city planning has not played any role at all in strategic planning because city planning is conceived of as being passive. It's just a platform for politics and economics. The city as player in politics and economics is not yet in the picture at all. I'm arguing that city planning can be active — it may not be as active as the other two arenas, but none the less, active to a certain degree.

CHAIRMAN

I think your concept of trying to design a city which is at peace with its environment is most exciting. If you can carry it through, it will be a major breakthrough; the rest will follow. This could be particularly so if you could concentrate, let's say, on the tropical city itself. In this light your ideas on the development of Kampong Bugis are right ones. You also have enough elbow room down there.

TAY KHENG SOON

The area is well defined. Also one of the technologies is to centralize the air-conditioning system. Sea water could be used for cooling and then tapping waste heat for desalination since it's a closed system. Now, that you can do when you are planning a large area. And yet of course every building when it taps on to the system will pay a sum to a central body which provides the central system. But each building must be a separate initiative.

QUESTION
Why do you advocate high-rise and high-density urban living? Isn't it better to go for low-energy and low-density living?

TAY KHENG SOON
I know that whole argument, and romantics like Theodore Roszak argue that very well in the book *Where the Wasteland Ends*. Throughout the last 200 years, there have been anti-city sentiments. But the fact is that urbanization has been on the increase everywhere in the world, and people want to live in cities. That's an undeniable fact despite all the ills cities have. So, I'm not very sure about the idea of dispersing into the countryside. People like Alvin Toffler and Marshall Macluhan talk about the "electronic cottage", the idea of teleworking from a distance. I think that the experiments so far have shown that the physical isolation of people from other people has been a problem. And teleworking mothers would tell of the need for companionship, of comradeship among fellow workers and so forth. Teleworking needs to be balanced by an appropriate social structure. And I think in the end that's the real reason for people living close together. There will always be those people — I think Roszak will be one of them, and probably some way-out environmentalists and naturalistic philoso-

Answer ignorer suburbs that have been growing more than cities. He's stuck E E, Howard's 2 mag

78

MEGA-CITIES IN THE TROPICS

phers and poets as well — those who like to live in a cottage somewhere out there. But I think most people find the company of other people quite enjoyable and quite useful. And that's the reason for cities. People want to get together, and ultimately that's what cities are for. Cities are information and commodity exchange systems — and exchange systems are at different levels — psychological exchange being one of them. So, I don't buy the idea that cities are going to be dispersed and people will move out. On the contrary, people are going to move more and more into cities, especially when the city is able to satisfy more and more dimensions of life. And that is why cities have to become better places. The Tropical City concept is just such a vision for the equatorial zone.

CLOSING REMARKS

CHAIRMAN

Tay Kheng Soon's presentation today forms part of a larger ongoing project on what would be the optimal urban design for the tropics. And every time Kheng Soon leads a discussion on it, he moves the idea forward — fleshes it out a bit and sets the stage for the next try. Needless to say, Kheng Soon, we are all glad with the progress you are making. At this rate we may, say a year hence, be ready to present your ideas to decision makers to see whether they will take to them, whether they will buy them. Till then all the best and thank you very much for a stimulating discussion.

THE AUTHOR

Tay Kheng Soon is a practising architect in Singapore with undertakings in Malaysia, Thailand, Mauritius, Brunei, and elsewhere. He writes and lectures besides his practice and was a Visiting Scholar at the Aga Khan Program at MIT in 1986 and 1989. He is also a Research Associate at the Institute of Southeast Asian Studies. Currently he has been nominated by the Singapore Institute of Architects to lead a team for an urban design study of Kampong Bugis where his ideas are being elaborated in a real context.

Tay's interest in the tropical city goes back to his student days in the 1960s at the Singapore Polytechnic School of Architecture where he was first introduced to the work of Maxwell Fry in Africa and to the construction of a sun-path diagram for Singapore. This experience sustained an interest in climate as an important generator of building form and life-style. It was therefore natural that in the quest for a modern Asian regional identity he focused on tropicality as the main theme. This theme was seen by him to subsume the other historical-stylistic references in the dialogues on architectural identity.

On the issuance of this book he would have completed a town-planning assignment by the Singapore Ministry of National Development on Kampong Bugis — a 72-hectare urban site as a tropical city for living and working in.